JAPANESE CASTLES

by Michio Fujioka

translated by
John Brentnall

edited by Don Kenny

Contents

Himeji Castle	4
Medieval Yamajiro (Mountain Castles)	7
Topographical Position of Castles	11
Hirayama-jiro (Hill Castles)	15
Hira-jiro (Castles Built on Flat Land)	18
Donjons of the Early Modern Period	22
Development of the Donjon	25
Architecture Adapted to Its Site	26
Strengthening the Defences	30
The Artistry of the Castle Donjon	35
The Castle Donjon in its Prime	39
The Maze-like Plan	43
The Defences Perfected	47
Collective Beauty	51
Edo Castle	55
Osaka Castle	59
The Central Donjons of the Edo Era	65
Rebuilding Castles under the Tokugawas	68
The Impressive Power of the Stone Walls	71
The Technique of Building Stone Walls	74
Tower Styles	78
Castle Gates	82
The Castle's White Walls	86
Castle Bridges	90
Entrance of the Main Donjon	93
The Tiled Roofs	94
Japanese and Western Castles	98
Outstanding Japanese Castles	106
The Plan of Japanese Castles (*Nawabari*)	113
Himeji Castle's Nawabari	118

JAPANESE CASTLES

by Michio Fujioka
translated by John Brentnall
edited by Don Kenny

© All rights reserved. No.12 of Hoikusha's Color Books Series. Published by Hoikusha Publishing Co., Ltd., 8-6, 4-chome, Tsurumi, Tsurumi-ku, Osaka, 538 Japan. ISBN 4-586-54012-5. First Edition in 1968. 14th Edition in 1993. Printed in JAPAN

Inuyama Castle (Hakutei Castle)

Himeji Castle from the east, after restoration

Himeji Castle

Himeji Castle was built in 1609 by Terumasa Ikeda who was appointed Lord of Harima district for meritorious service in the Sekigahara War (1600). It is the finest remaining example of a Japanese castle, and was closed for 8 years from 1956 to enable skilful restoration work to preserve its unique beauty.

Terumasa, greatly trusted son-in-law of Ieyasu Tokugawa, the ruling Shogun, built the castle at Himeji as a defence against the western lords who were pressing for revolt against

Himeji Castle
from the north-east,
before restoration

the Tokugawa government. With strong government support and an annual stipend of 180,000 kiloliters of rice, Terumasa built a castle ranking in magnificence with those of Edo and Osaka.

Built at a time when the technique of castle construction was at its peak, it surpasses all other castles in every respect. The special white clay, used for the first time on its walls, is not only fireproof but adds greatly to its beauty. It is also known as Shirasagi Castle (White Heron Castle) as its appearance gives the effect of a great white bird in flight.

Mt. Gagyu on which Takahashi Castle is built

Medieval Yamajiro (Mountain Castles)

During medieval days most Japanese castles were built on mountains or at the protective base of a mountain to ensure an advantageous position in event of attack. The choice of such a position became less frequent when the castle became the center of the political and economic life of the district. The House of Matsuura, pictured below, is one of the old strategically-positioned mansions which was used long after the medieval period.

The House of Matsuura at Hirado

Takahashi Castle, the donjon

Takahashi Castle (Matsuyama Castle) is built on the thickly wooded summit of Mt. Gagyu in Takahashi City, Okayama Prefecture. It is important as the only remaining example of a medieval yamajiro which has a donjon. In a yamajiro it was not necessary to make the donjon high, and this donjon has only ni-ju (two stories). In those days superstition prohibited the building of a donjon with an even number of stories, so a mezzanine floor was built and it was known as a san-ju (three storied tower). The castle was restored by Katsumune Mizutani in 1681.

In Takeda City, Oita Prefecture, is another Mt. Gagyu atop of which stands Oka Castle. This is another interesting medieval yamajiro which was used after medieval days despite its mountain top position. Built in 1185 by the Ogata family, the Nakagawa family captured it in 1594 and since then seventeen generations of this family have lived there. This is the castle made famous by Rentaro Taki's song, Kojo No Tsuki (Moon over the Deserted Castle).

The inner citadel of Oka Castle

Karatsu Castle, The stone wall on the east side

The land features surrounding Hirado Castle

Topographical Position of Castles

The natural features of the land were all used to advantage when building a castle. Mountains, rivers, lakes and the sea were often integrated into the defence plans. Both Karatsu Castle and Hirado Castle make use of the sea as a big moat. To make the castle less vulnerable to attack a position with complicated land features was preferred, so the castles often commanded superb views and the central donjon was built in a position which gave a complete panorama of the surrounding countryside.

It was the rule to build a castle where the immediate land features were most suitable for defence. However, as the castle became the center of the political and economic life of its district, it became necessary to consider not only the immediate vicinity but also the surrounding towns and villages.

Hagi Castle, on page 13, made exceptionally good use of the surrounding land features. The castle town was built on a delta with the castle standing guard on a headland facing the sea. This isolated and unapproachable site was specially chosen by Terumoto Mori after his defeat in the Sekigahara War (1600).

Karatsu Castle was also built in a strategic position. It stands on the tip of a small peninsula, and by constructing a system of moats it was cut off from the mainland. This was built by Hirotaka Terasawa at the close of the 16th century.

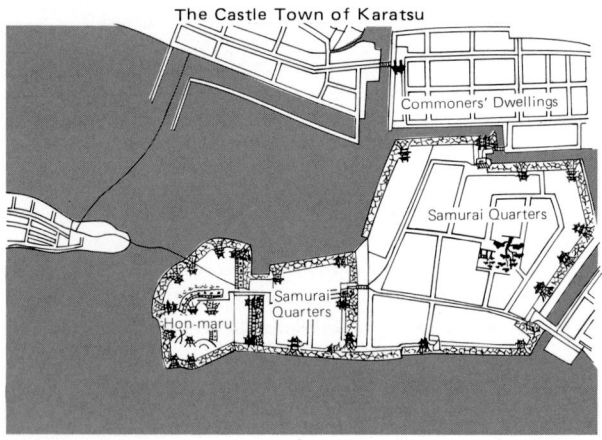

The Castle Town of Karatsu

The Castle Town of Hagi

These strongholds have not been developed in any way, and as time went on the population of Hagi decreased while that of Osaka and Edo greatly increased. Thus, as the rôle of the castle changed, it became increasingly difficult to decide whether to plan to construct a castle chiefly as a fortress or as the center of the life of the community.

Wakayama Castle, after rebuilding

Hirayama-jiro (Hill Castles)

Wakayama Castle is a typical hirayama-jiro. The characteristics of an early Modern Period castle are caught in this picture taken from the town below.

Himeji Castle from the west

It was in the hirayama-jiro that the true beauty of a Japanese castle was fully made manifest. In this type of castle the innermost citadel was built on a hill and the second and third citadels were built on the slopes of the hill. Himeji Castle is the outstanding example of this type.

Himeyama, the hill on which Himeji Castle stands, has a steep northern slope, so it is on the gentler southern slope that the outer citadels are scattered making a truly magnificent sight. If the outer citadels of Wakayama Castle were extant it would rival Himeji in grandeur. Unfortunately, many castles have now lost their outer citadels and only the central citadel remains to remind us of their former magnificence. If the hirayama-jiro was built on a high hill it resembled a yama-jiro; such is the case with Matsuyama Castle in Ehime Prefecture, Shikoku. On the other hand, if the hill was low, the hirayama-jiro takes on the nature of a hira-jiro (castle built on flat land) as in the case of Edo and Osaka castles.

As time progressed the castle became the symbol of the daimyo's (lord's) power and authority, and the hirayama-jiro built in a position which dominated the surrounding area, filled this role perfectly.

Himeji Castle from the north

Hira-jiro (castles built on flat land)

This type of castle was not as scenically impressive as the hirayama-jiro, but being easy of access it was more convenient as the castle became the center of the life of the community.

Matsumoto Castle

Nijo Castle, Kyoto
The entrance and front moat

Nagoya Castle

Castles built on flat land increased as the castle became the administrative center of the district. Although its position was more convenient, it had serious strategic disadvantages. Attempts were made at a much more diversified system of fortification so that Hakone, for example, was the frontier fortress of Edo Castle. In general the hira-jiro could be planned with much greater flexibility as it did not depend upon the surrounding land features. It is true, however, that in the castle building itself the question of defence continued to be a major consideration.

Nijo Castle in Kyoto had a rather exceptional character as

Takamatsu Castle

it was principally used to accommodate the Tokugawa generals on their frequent visits to the capital, Kyoto. Jurakudai, Hideyoshi Toyotomi's mansion, was used for similar purposes.

Nagoya Castle was started by Ieyasu Tokugawa in 1610 for his son, Yoshinao. Although built on a plain, it was heavily fortified in every direction except the north which provided its own protection in the form of a swamp.

Takamatsu Castle, Shikoku, built by the Ikoma family in 1587, was later restored by the Matsudaira family. Again a hira-jiro, but with the added protection of surrrounding water.

The central donjon of Hiroshima Castle, after rebuilding

Donjons of the Early Modern Period

At this stage of development the donjon had wooden walls, "push-out" windows and a small turret. Whilst affecting a certain lightness it lacked the grace and ostentation of the later Modern Period.

The donjon of Kumamoto Castle

The donjon of Inuyama Castle

The donjon of Maruoka Castle

The interior of Okayama Castle's donjon (before destruction by fire)

Development of the Donjon

The central architectural feature of the castle is the donjon or castle tower. This was first introduced in Azuchi Castle at the end of the Muromachi Period (1576). It began as a small observation turret built on the roof, and gradually developed into a many-storied donjon. The donjons of Inuyama and Maruoka castles show the earliest features, whilst the donjons of Hiroshima and Kumamoto show the developed features. As the above picture of Okayama Castle shows, the earlier donjons had a room at the top which was often used for meetings by the lord of the castle. The simplicity of the wooden walls and "push-out" windows are also characteristics of this style of donjon.

The donjon of Wakayama Castle, after rebuilding

Architecture Adapted to its Site

On the first floor of Wakayama Castle most corners of the building are curved. This is due to the small area of the hill-top on which it is built. Planning the effective use of such a small area for a castle must have been a very complicated task.

Wakayama Castle, the watch tower after rebuilding

Wakayama Castle, Kusunoki Gate after rebuilding

Wakayama Castle, small tower

As Japan lies in a volcanic region most of its mountains and hills tend to be volcanic in shape. These pointed peaks caused many problems when constructing a hill castle. The architecture of a hirayama-jiro was often irregular owing to the limited space on the hill top and the difficulties of building on the steep slopes of the hill. A massive, rectangular stone-wall base was first constructed and the castle built on top of this. In early days the construction of this rectangular base was difficult even on flat land, and building it on the peak of a conical hill really tested the ingenuity of the castle planners.

The inner citadel of Wakayama Castle was built on this kind of peak. Despite reclamation work and cutting away sections of the hill-top the area was so limited that all corners of the building are curved. The small tower, seen in the picture, is built on an irregular, pentagonal first storey.

Kochi Castle, intersecting roofs of the tower

Recently very simple plans of this castle were found. These were apparently used during restoration work at the end of the Edo era. In the early days it seems they worked from only very rough plans as it was impossible for them to make detailed plans on such irregular terrain.

In Wakayama Castle the first storey of the central donjon was rhombic, and that of Okayama Castle (destroyed by fire) was irregular pentagonal. In such cases the roofs of the lower buildings demanded careful planning as the intricate construction in the picture illustrates.

Construction of the rectangular stone base became less difficult as techniques improved. Later, when the hira-jiro was developed, the flat site presented none of the former problems, so these irregular structures became less frequent.

Kumamoto Castle, the central donjon after rebuilding

Strengthening the Defences

In both Kumamoto Castle and Matsumoto Castle it became evident that the central donjon was to be used for practical defence purposes, and it assumed a more fortified appearance.

Matsumoto Castle, the central donjon

Kumamoto Castle, the central donjon (right), and the small tower after rebuilding

In its early development the main purpose of the central donjon was to symbolize the power and authority of the lord of the castle, but it also had the function of a watch-tower. Later, it continued to symbolize authority, but it also developed into the strongly fortified main artery of the castle's defence system.

Azuchi Castle very well exemplifies the donjon in its early role. The rooms on each storey were splendidly decorated by the famous painter Eitoku Kano, and the exterior walls were impressively adorned with red and gold plaster.

As the wars between the ruling families became more severe, the main donjon was gradually fortified and used for defence purposes. The main donjon of Kumamoto Castle, for example, was built on foundation supports which extended over the stone-wall base. (See picture on page 32).

This was done in order to make the first storey rectangular, and this additional space was used as a stone-throwing area. The small tower of Kumamoto Castle, built after the main donjon, clearly shows the increased number of stone-throwing "windows". An added deterrent for wall-scalers was the introduction of an iron-spiked fence along the edge of the stone wall.

The donjon of Matsumoto Castle, begun in 1594 and completed in 1597, also had stone-throwing "windows". These were situated not only at each corner of the first storey, but also in the middle of each outside wall.

Later developements within the main donjon compound included the construction of wells, kitchens, toilets, etc., for use in case of seige. Thus the castle donjon developed, and although the donjon walls were wooden they bristled with various types of fortification.

Matsumoto Castle,
the stone-throwing windows
in the donjon

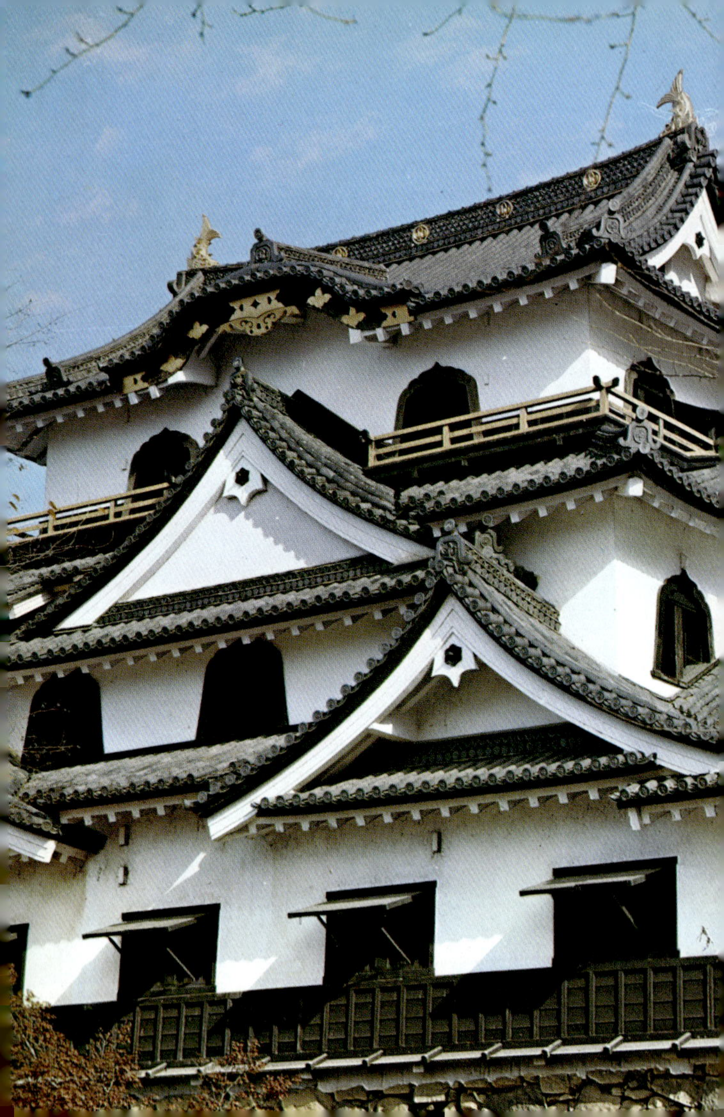

◀ Hikone Castle, detailed view of gables

The Artistry of the Castle Donjon

Despite the complexity of design, the main donjon of Hikone Castle is a fine tribute to the skill and artistry of the builders. The harmoniously intersecting gables and the many bell-shaped windows are its chief features. These finely shaped windows were introduced to make the interior of the castle brighter.

Hikone Castle, the main donjon

During the Tensho period (1573-1591) a castle was built in Otsu, but in 1606, under the orders of Naotsugu Ii, the central citadel and donjon were moved to Hikone. During the course of removal certain alterations and restoration work were inevitable, but it undoubtedly retains many of the characteristics of the castles of the Tensho period. In appearance the castle donjon is both complex and unique. The general structure of the early castle donjons was to build the tower on the main roof which had curved, sweeping gables. Hikone Castle is built according to this general plan, but many gables were added to the main roof. It is in the skilful interlacing of these various gables that the technical artistry lies, creating a castle at once strong in structure and elegant in appearance.

If Hikone Castle's artistry lies in its skilful design, the artistry of Nagoya Castle lies in its many practical devices. Completed by Ieyasu Tokugawa in 1613, it lacks the graceful lines and elegance of Hikone Castle. Simple in design and more rigid in line, it is nevertheless equipped with many clever military devices. Inside the stone walls are secret storerooms for rice, money, etc., and wells were dug for use when the castle was beseiged. The hidden interstices and stone-throwing "windows" are especially noteworthy. The hidden interstices are located just below the first floor windows. They were concealed by a thin covering which was painted like the walls, and when needed the thin covering was broken from inside the castle. The stone-throwing "windows" were also unobservable from the outside. They were built under the protruding walls just below the gables, and the "windows" opened underneath the thick eaves.

Thus, Nagoya Castle was often compared to a cat hiding her Sharp claws.

Nagoya Castle, the donjon before destruction by fire

Himeji Castle, the donjon seen from Gate 'Ni' (D)

Himeji Castle, seen from Hishi Gate

The Castle Donjon in its Prime

Built when the art of castle construction was in its prime, Himeji Castle is overwhelming in its beauty and grandeur. It is unique, and in no other country can such a castle be seen. Its elevation and pure white walls lend a grace and distinction never-to-be-forgotten, yet its magnificence is not the result of external decoration but stems from the harmony and excellence of its design.

South side of Himeji Castle donjon, after restoration

Castle construction in Japan flourished most during the 15 years between the Sekigahara War (1600) and the Osaka War (1614). It is said that when Himeji Castle was completed in 1609 some 25 other castles were being constructed in various parts of Japan. Both Himeji Castle and Matsue Castle (page 41) were built during this prosperous period; the former is white and the latter is black.

Matsue Castle was built in 1611 by Yoshiharu Horii who was rewarded for meritorious service in the Sekigahara War. Because of its dark appearance it is sometimes compared to an

Matsue Castle Donjon

old samurai with black strings on his armor, whilst the elegant Himeji Castle is likened to a young samurai with red strings on his armor. Although differing considerably in size, the basic structure of these two castles is similar. Both have a three-storied tower on top of big, double roofs, but their towers differ in structure. These two castles, together with Hagi Castle which was destroyed at the beginning of the Meiji era, exemplify the beauty of the castle donjon in its prime period of construction.

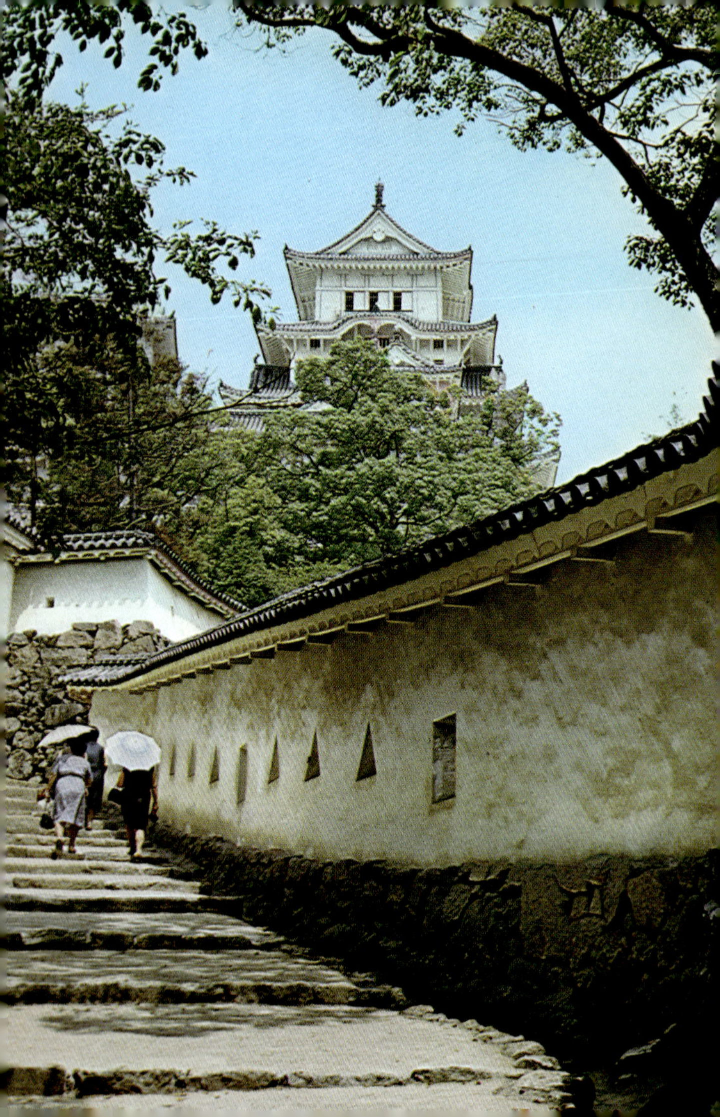

The Maze-like Plan

No ancient castle is complete without its maze, and in the case of Himeji Castle this has been integrated into the general plan of the castle. The way from Gate C to D is so labyrinth-like that even though the donjon appears to be very near it takes much time to reach it.

◀ Himeji Castle donjon and the approach to Gate 'Ha' (C)

Himeji Castle, The maze-like approach to Gate D

See pages 102-103 of text. Let us consider for a moment Himeji Castle which has one of the most complicated plans.

A narrow, sloping path between walls continues from Gate A and passing through Gate C makes a 180° turn and proceeds to Gate D. In front of each gate the road narrows to prevent large numbers of the enemy entering simultaneously during an attack. Passing through Gate D the path continues to the hidden Gate E which is very low and is under a wall. If we continue to follow the road we shall by-pass the main donjon and arrive at the back gate of the castle! In order to reach the main donjon, after passing through Gate E we must immediately turn right and pass through First Water Gate. Such maze-like twists and corners must have been greatly effective in confusing an enemy who had gained entrance to the castle.

Himeji Castle, Gate 'Ho' (E) at right, and Suiitsu-Mon (First Water Gate) at left

Himeji Castle, Gate 'Ho' (E)

45

Himeji Castle, Gate 'Ni' (D)

The Defences Perfected

Part of the maze-like plan of Himeji Castle was the construction of many gates to confuse the enemy. There are 21 gates altogether. Between the main donjon and the small northwest tower is a kitchen in the courtyard, so they could withstand a seige from the main donjon alone. The defences were perfect.

Himeji Castle, the small Inui Tower (Northwest Tower)

Himeji Castle, Suigo no Mon (Fifh Water Gate)

Himeji Castle, the small northwest tower and the kitchen below

The central donjon of Himeji Castle was so strongly and effectively fortified that they could hold the castle from there even when beseiged. The final gate to the central donjon, Suigo no Mon (Fifth Water Gate), on page 48, is located under the bridging tower between the main donjon and the small west tower. Its doors and supporting pillars are completely covered with iron and the stone-throwing "windows" just above the gate are open. Passing through Suigo no Mon and under the small north-west tower we come into the courtyard where the "seige" kitchen is located. As there was little danger of enemy attack here, the windows facing the courtyard were made larger to afford better interior lighting. In this point we find a modern rationalism creeping into the construction. The courtyard could hold many soldiers.

Himeji Castle, the donjon from the south-east

The west citadel of Himeji Castle seen from the moat Sangoku (Three Prefectures)

Himeji Castle, the donjon from the south-west

Collective Beauty

The beauty and magnificence of Himeji Castle is not created by any one particular building, but by the aspect presented by all the buildings collectively. If the central donjon were isolated from the other buildings it would lose in magnificence. Each building plays a part in adding to the collective beauty of the whole.

Matsuyama Castle, the donjon and Shichiku Mon

Iyo-Matsuyama Castle in Ehime Prefecture was built in 1602 by Yoshiaki Kato. After restoration in 1642 the central donjon was destroyed by lightning. In 1854 it was rebuilt and its black, wooden walls resemble the original building. Although not as magnificent as Himeji Castle, the large number of remaining gates and towers collectively make an impressive array.

Matsuyama Castle, Kintetsu Mon (Iron-Strength Gate)

Matsuyama Castle, Ichi no Mon (No. 1. Gate)

53

Edo Castle, the stone wall atop its high bank

Edo Castle, Hirakawa Gate

Edo Castle

Edo Castle, home of the Tokugawa Shoguns, was the largest castle in Japan. Most of the buildings have been destroyed, but a few gates remain to hint of its former grandeur. The combination of stone wall set on a high bank foundation was uncommon.

Edo Castle, Sakashita Mon from inside the castle grounds

Ieyasu Tokugawa built "the unparalleled under the heavens" Edo Castle. After defeating the Hojo family in the Odawara War, Ieyasu was appointed daimyo of the Kanto area (today's Kanto Plains surrounding Tokyo). The general opinion of the day was that he would continue to use the Hojo family's military headquarters in Odawara, or perhaps move to Kamakura which had been the capital in the Kamakura era (1192–1321). Instead, after consulting Hideyoshi, Ieyasu chose the small town of Edo as his military base. Edo had a small castle built by Ota Dokan, head of the Uesugi family. The people were very surprised at Ieyasu's choice of this comparatively unknown town as in those days Edo was a swampy, reed-bestrewn region with no place to build either a castle town or even adequate quarters for his samurai (retainers).

All the reasons for his choise are not known, but it is

Edo Castle, Fushimi Tower

certain that he fully appreciated the importance of Edo's position as being convenient for travel both by sea and land. Ieyasu's foresight in this choice has since been proved as Edo quickly developed into a big city, and, as Tokyo, is now the largest city in the world!

After Ieyasu became Shogun in 1603, Edo expanded very rapidly. By then the inner citadel and the west and north citadels of his castle had been completed. The central donjon must have been magnificent, but unfortunately all records have been lost and no source remains to suggest its architectural appearance. It is known that during the Kan-ei era (1624-43) the central donjon was rebuilt, but after being destroyed by fire in 1657 it was not rebuilt again. Today only a few towers and gates are preserved, but only one or two of these date back to the early Edo era.

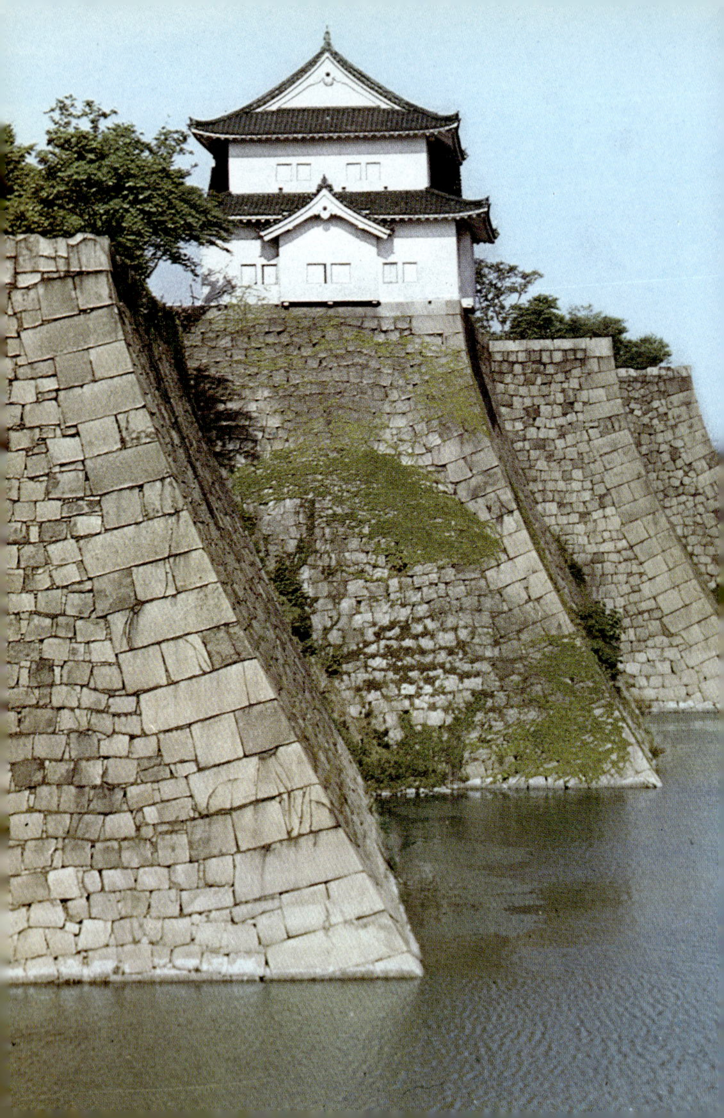

◀ Osaka Castle,
the moat
and stone walls

Osaka Castle

The castle which remains today was built by the Tokugawa family. The original castle built by the Toyotomi family was deliberately destroyed and the present castle was built from a completely new plan. (see next page)

Osaka Castle, Sakura Gate (Cherry Blossom Gate)

Osaka Castle was first built by Hideyoshi Toyotomi in 1583 after his victory in the Shizugatake War. As chief Daimyo (lord) he ruled all Japan until his death in 1598, but his castle was almost completely destroyed in the Osaka Wars (1614-15). Ieyasu Tokugawa, after his victory in these wars, commanded the daimyos of the west to rebuild the castle after a completely new plan. The Tokugawa government made great efforts to have the castle completed as they regarded it as their frontier fortress in controlling the western districts of Japan.

In recent years the original plan of the castle which Hideyoshi built was found, and when compared with the remains of the castle built by the Tokugawa family, many details were completely different. Although the inner citadel and the moat are located in the same place, many stone walls had been replanned and built in different locations. The original stone walls could have been repaired and used, but the

Osaka Castle, Sengan (Precious) Tower and Inui (north-west) Tower

fact that they were destroyed and new ones built in new locations is evidence of the Tokugawa family's policy after the Sekigahara Wars to exterminate all trace of the Toyotomi family and their achievements.

There remain several original towers and gates in today's Osaka Castle, and the oldest is the Inui (north-west) Tower. It was probably built in 1620 by the Tokugawas. The central donjon was built in 1626 but was destroyed by lightning in 1665.

The main donjon which stands today was rebuilt in 1931, and as though in tribute to both families it stands on the Tokugawa castle's foundations, but was built to resemble a picture of the Toyotomi Castle. However, today's Osaka Castle has an elevator and architectural details not in accord with historical research.

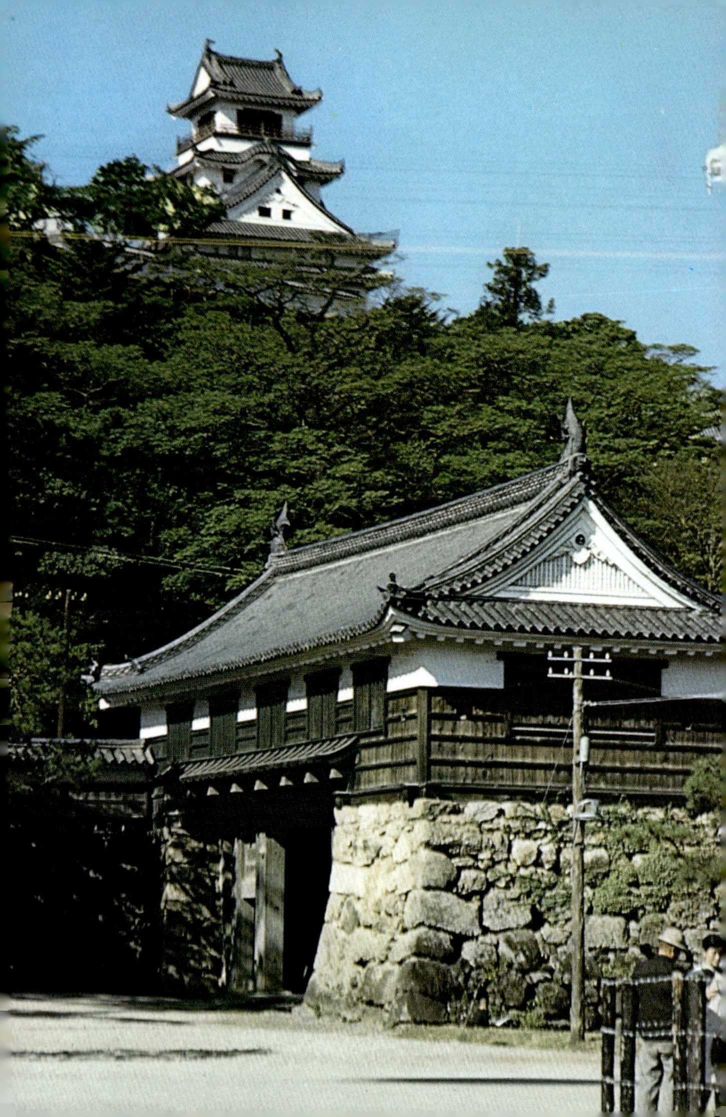

Uwajima Castle, the main donjon

◀ Kochi Castle, Shikoku, the front gate and main donjon

63

Fukuyama Castle, Hiroshima Prefecture.
The main donjon before destruction by fire

Mito Castle, the main donjon before destruction by fire

The Central Donjons of the Edo Era

In the Edo era some donjons were rebuilt in the old style, but others were constructed with entirely new influences in the design.

The main donjon of Kochi Castle was rebuilt in 1747. Although certain details are new, on the whole it is built in the old style and greatly resembles Inuyama Castle.

Uwajima Castle, rebuilt in 1662 by Munetoshi Date, is a typical example of the Edo style castle.

Fukuyama Castle also exemplifies the new style of the Edo era. Built in 1622 by Katsunari Mizuno, this castle was used as a base for controlling the western provinces.

The central donjon of Mito Castle was rebuilt soon after it had been destroyed by fire in 1764. Compared with the flowing lines of earlier castles this has a very austere, box-like appearance, which typified another Edo style.

The various styles of donjons which were built in the Edo era reflect the varying and changing social conditions of that age. Uwajima Castle was built in a completely new style, Kochi Castle retained the old style, but Matsuyama Castle and Hirosaki Castle combined both styles.

Hirosaki Castle, the main donjon

Matsuyama Castle, the central donjon ▶

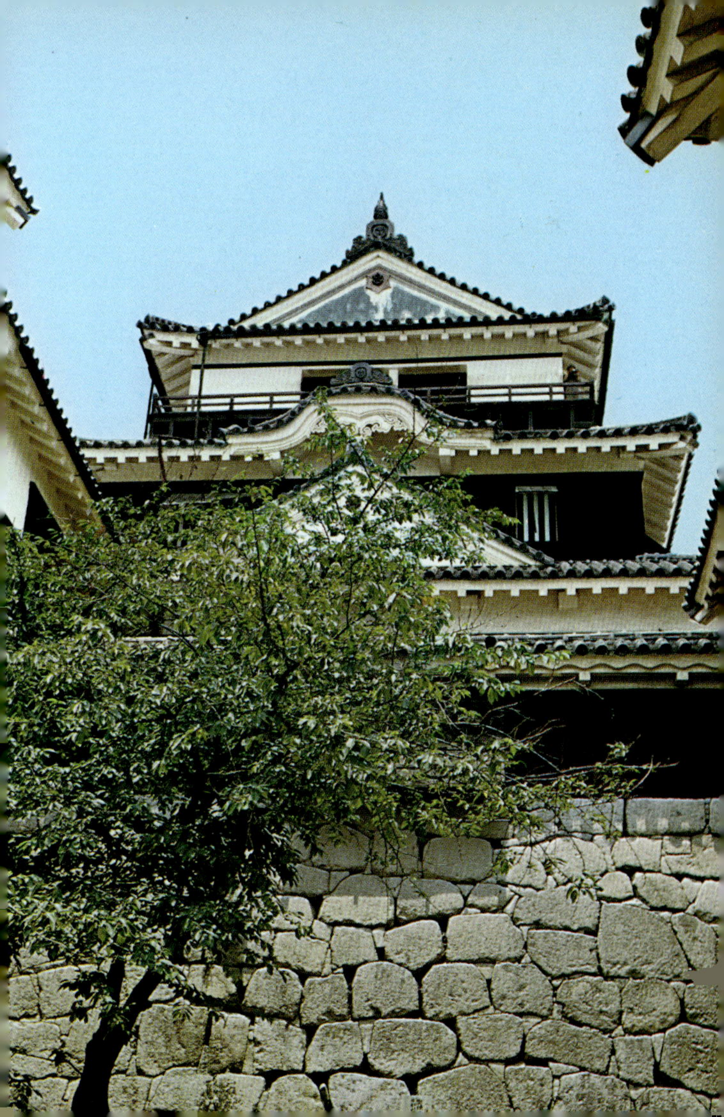

Kochi Castle, the central donjon

Rebuilding Castles under the Tokugawas

The Tokugawa government brought a period of relative peace and stability to Japan and many daimyos applied to the government for permission to rebuild their war-torn castles. Permission was usually granted depending upon the government's own defence policies, and according to the principle that any rebuilding should follow the original style of the particular castle. Thus it was that much rebuilding work done in Edo days followed the old style. As the Tokugawa government did not reconstruct the central donjon of Edo castle many daimyos hesitated to rebuild theirs, and even when allowed to do so it was no longer called a donjon but just a tower, sanju (three-storied tower).

Wakayama Castle, the main donjon after rebuilding

The central donjon of Hirosaki Castle was rebuilt in 1810, but its scale and location are so completely different from the original, it is virtually a new castle. Only the many interstices in its walls (p. 66) reflect the old style.

Iyo-Matsuyama Castle's central donjon has a very new appearance. but its wooden walls and "push out" windows follow the old tradition. This was probably done so that it should harmonize with the surrounding castle buildings when it was rebuilt in 1854.

The main donjon of Wakayama Castle was rebuilt in 1850 on the foundations of the original castle. Thus it retains many of the original features such as its irregularity in design, stone throwing "windows", etc., but it adopted the new style in certain details.

Nagoya Castle, the bridging stone wall between the main donjon and the small tower

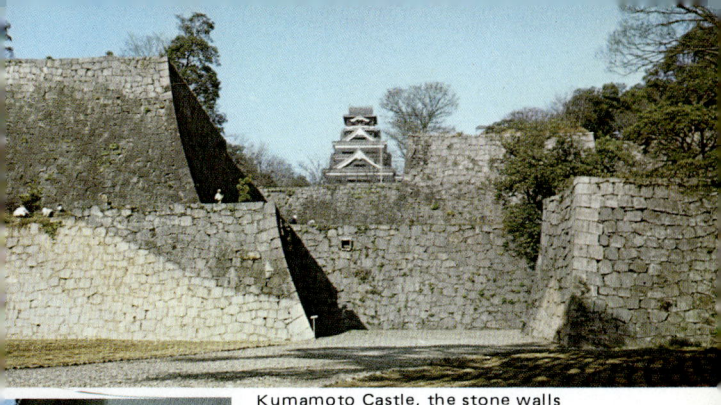

Kumamoto Castle, the stone walls

The Impressive Power of the Stone Walls

Few can stand before the mighty stone walls of a Japanese castle and fail to be impressed by their rugged beauty and power. Although oblivious of the efforts of the thousands of workmen, or the demands of the lord who compelled this labor, one cannot deny their mysterious power.

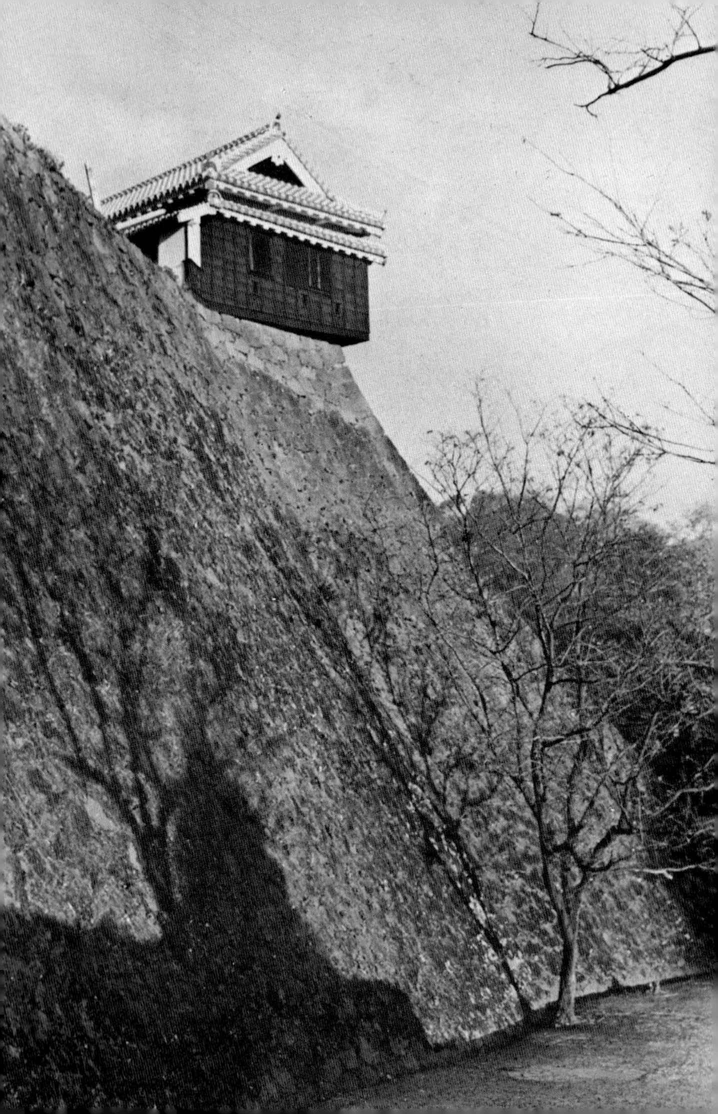

The stone wall is such an impressive feature of a Japanese castle that whenever the latter is spoken of, the former is always remembered. Stone, considered in Japan to be eternal, is used in Japanese as a synonym for "strength", "firmness", thus the wall evokes a masculine force. This force was indispensable, especially when the castle not only symbolized the power and authority of the lord but also became a fortress.

Near Sakura Mon (Cherry Blossom Gate) of Osaka Castle there is a stone so huge that we wonder how it was moved. Such a huge stone had no real practical purpose, but was used to display its force and power. This is evident from the fact that such huge stones were usually placed near the front gate.

The stone wall of a castle, like the sea, holds fascination of which one never tires.

Hirosaki Castle, the stone wall

The Technique of Building Stone Walls

There are various kinds of stone wall such as high, straight, curved, gently-sloped, steeply-sloped, etc., and each has its specific function. To understand these functions is to realize the wisdom of the builders of past eras.

Himeji Castle, the stone wall near Gate C

Himeji Castle, the stone wall below Taiko (Drum) Tower

Hagi Castle, the stone wall below the main donjon

To the casual observer the natural stones in the huge walls seem to have been piled up haphazardly, but that they still stand firm today, centuries after construction, proves the excellence of the building technique. These techniques must have been learned only through experience, but in the light of modern scientific knowledge we are often surprised at the logic behind the methods.

For example, the stone walls beneath the central donjons of both Kumamoto and Hagi castles have very gently curving slopes extending to their wide bases, but beneath the watching tower of Kumamoto Castle (p. 73) the wall is steeper and less curved. At first sight this may seem strange, but the builders considered not only the weight of the building on top of the

Tsuyama Castle, the massive corner stones of the wall

wall, but also the solidity of the wall's foundations. The main donjon usually stands on the highest ground. Therefore the distance to the solid substratum is further, also it is usually the biggest building in the castle, so the wall beneath it needs the widest base. In the case of the watching-tower the distance to the solid substratum is not so far and the small tower is much lighter in weight than the main donjon, therefore a wide base was unnecessary.

Thus from the manner of construction of the stone walls we can judge the firmness of the substratum below. One cannot help admiring the people of old who developed these techniques.

Tower Styles

Towers were built at strategically important points of the castle. Although smaller in scale than the main donjon, the structure was essentially the same. The Inui Tower of Osaka Castle (p. 79) has the unusual feature of a first and second storey of equal size. This is the oldest tower in Osaka Castle.

Hikone Castle, Sanju (Three-storied) Tower in the west citadel

Osaka Castle, Inui (North-West) Tower

Takamatsu Castle, Tsukimi (waching the arrival) Tower

Matsumoto Castle, Tsukimi (moon-viewing) Tower

The tower names varied along with the styles, and perhaps one of the most unusual is Matsumoto Castle's Tsukimi Tower (below) built for the leisurely pursuit of moon viewing. It is completely open on the east and south sides, and in style resembles a palace rather than a castle. In this sense it is unique to find the soft lines of palace architecture combined with the more dignified structure of a castle.

Tsukimi Tower in Takamatsu Castle (above) was built overlooking the sea to watch the arrival and departure of ships. It is sometimes confused with the previous tower owing to the same name (the way of writing the names in Japanese is different), but it is less elegant in both structure and function than the

Shibata Castle, the two-storied tower in the inner citadel

moon-viewing tower.

Other unique towers, designed like the moon-viewing tower with the ladies of the castle in mind, are the Suzumi (cooling oneself) Tower in Oka Castle, and the Kesho (cosmetics) Tower in Himeji Castle. This last was used by Princess Sen famed throughout the land for her beauty.

Generally speaking the towers have two or three stories and were built at important points such as the corner of a stone wall.

A long, rectangular shaped tower, called Tamon, was sometimes built. The Tamon Tower in Himeji Castle was used by the maidservants as a living room.

Castle Gates

Strategically the main point of entry, the castle gate was often surrounded by various devices for defence, but as the entrance to the castle it also had to be sufficiently imposing and decorative.

Kanazawa Castle, Ishikawa Gate

Himeji Castle, Hishi Gate

Nijo Castle, Front Gate

Edo Castle, Hanzo Gate

The entrance area of a Japanese castle is usually rectangular in shape and has two gates. This is called in Japanese masugata which means "the shape of a masu". A masu is a rectangular rice container which was similar in shape to the entrance area.

The entrance area was surrounded by a stone wall and had gates on two adjacent sides of the rectangle. One enters the castle from outside through the Korai (Korean) Gate, then one must turn right to pass through the second gate, the Tower Gate, which is on an inner wall. The entrance gates were thus designed so that the inside of the castle grounds could not be seen directly from outside.

The Korai Gate, as pictured above, has roofs on the supporting pillars, and these roofs inside the gate are characteristic of a castle gate. The Tower Gate is located under a bridging tower, hence its name, and usually has stone walls on both sides.

The masu-gata entrance was fully developed during the Keicho era (1596-1614) when the technique of castle construction itself was at its peak. Prior to this there had been a rectangular entrance area, but only one gate.

Another unusual type of gate is the Uzumi (Secret) Gate (page 45), but the masu-gata entrance is the most imposing type for a castle.

Matsuyama Castle, Tsutsui Mon

Kanazawa Castle, Namako (sea cucumber) wall

The Castle's White Walls

The long, white, roofed walls, together with the long walls of the Tamon Towers, play no small part in adding to the beauty of the castle.

However strong the stone walls supporting the castle may be, when topped by the long, low white walls the two combine to evoke a mysterious grandeur and beauty. The simple lines of the white walls themselves, extending for a long distance, create a strange feeling of strength.

Himeji Castle, west citadel wall seen from Kesho Tower

Osaka Castle, its white walls and interstices for cannons

The castle's long, white, roofed walls and the long walls of the Tamon Tower are always beautiful. In older castles these long walls were often made of wood and were black. The many long walls of Himeji Castle greatly enhance its beauty, but the black wooden fences of Kumamoto Castle and the "Namako" fence of Kanazawa Castle also evoke their own special beauty.

The walls of Himeji Castle are so thick that buttresses are unnecessary, but generally the wall had either wooden or stone buttresses as shown in the pictures.

Interstices for arrows and guns were often made in the walls, and at strategic points interstices for stone-throwing, too. Himeji Castle has many interestingly designed interstices, including round and triangular shapes.

In Osaka Castle there are interstices for cannons just below the white walls, pictured above.

Iyo-Matsuyama Castle, stone wall and stone-throwing windows

Kanazawa Castle, wooden buttresses supporting the white walls

Castle Bridges

The bridge over the dry, or water-filled moat, was an added protection for the main gate of the castle. In Europe most of these were drawbridges which could be drawn up in case of attack, but in Japan this type of bridge is very rare. This is probably because the bridges in Japan were completely made of wood and the difficult technique of drawbridges was never developed.

Edo Castle, the drawbridge on the north side

Hikone Castle, Tenbin (Symmetrical) Tower and bridge

Matsue Castle, entrance to the main donjon

Entrance of the Main Donjon

The phases of the times are evident, too, in the varying styles of entrance to the main donjon.

Matsue Castle's main donjon has an entrance completely covered with iron, like that of Himeji Castle, and stone throwing wndows protect both its sides. Such heavy fortification indicates that it was constructed in the Keicho era when the main donjon was used as a fortress.

The central donjon of Wakayama Castle, however, was rebuilt at the end of the Edo period. It has a strongly protected outer entrance (below left), but its wide, elegant inner entrance, which faces the courtyard, reveals the peaceful time during which it was built. The great contrast between these two entrances is an interesting feature.

Wakayama Castle, entrance to the main donjon after rebuilding

Matsuyama Castle, the roofs of various buildings

The Tiled Roofs

The many complex roof patterns add great architectural interest to Japanese castles. The straight lines of the Chidori (plover) gables, contrasting with the graceful curves of the Kara (Chinese Tang-Dynasty 626-907) gables (p. 34) are an important element in the beauty of the central donjon. In addition, the bold lines of the Japanese tiles on the various roofs and gates, topped by the figure of a leaping dolphin, add a movement and grace of line which make the Japanese castle unique.

Kochi Castle, the roof tiles and leaping dolphin

Hirosaki Castle, coppr-tiled roof

Generally the castle roof was tiled with thick, blue-grey Japanese clay tiles, but in the very early days some castles had thatched roofs. According to an extant photograph, the central donjon of Shinshu-Takashima Castle was thatched with shingles, as was Iwakuni Castle which was constructed as late as 1602.

In the cold, northern districts the usual clay tiles were used, and in Hirosaki Castle (see picture) copper tiles were used. Lead tiles were also used in some castles.

In both structure and design Japanese tiles are an important element in all Japanese architecture, and the beauty of the roofs is especially dominant in Japanese castles.

Japanese Castles

Japanese and Western Castles

The name castle has been given to a great variety of buildings in Japan in different ages. Historic ruins of some of the earliest types can still be seen in northern Honshu and in Hokkaido Japan's northern-most island.

In ancient times the Ainu aborigines built stockades on mountain tops and called them "*chyashi*", the Ainu word for castle. Remains of large mansions called "tachi", in northern Honshu, provide evidence that these were used for entertaining Imperial and other high-ranking guests. During the Nara period (7th century) invasions from Korea and China necessitated the building of frontier fortifications on southern Honshu and Kyushu. Two types remain; Korean style mountain castles and "mizuki", water castles, which were completely surrounded by wide moats. The ancient capitals of Nara and Kyoto, as homes of the early emperors, were developed into the first castle towns. Later, in northern Honshu, a series of castle forts was constructed.

These different types of castles reflected the needs of the times, and by the beginning of the Middle Ages (1192) the castle had become a fortress for use in time of war. With the decline of the emperor's power and the rise of powerful family clans, power struggles ensued resulting in bitter wars between rival families. They planned their estates accordingly. Sites offering natural defence were chosen, and it was usual for them to have a manor house for peacetime, and a mountain castle to which they could retreat when attacked.

By the beginning of the 17th century Japan had developed into a strongly feudal society. The leader of the most powerful family was the military ruler (*shogun*), governing numerous country lords (*daimyo*), each with his own castle and band of retainers (*samurai*). During this period the role of the castle changed phenomenally from the fortress of the Middle Ages to the dignified residence of the local daimyo. It became the centre of the political and economic life of the district, and reflected the lord's power and influence in its grace of line and imposing architecture.

This harmonizing of the external appearance not only gave the Japanese castle a new-found splendor, but also a completely new status in the field of architecture. These are the castles of real architectural worth and it is such castles that are often compared with Western medieval castles.

The comparison is interesting: as the lord's residence their function was naturally similar, but in construction there is a fundamental difference. Traditionally Japan was a country of wooden buildings and castle construction did not deviate from this tradition. If we eliminate the few special materials used in some castles, they are, in fact, completely wooden structures. Compared with the stone and brick castles of the West, these wooden castles were not only less durable and fire-resistant, they also lacked structural solidity. The thick stone walls of Western castles could of themselves hold an enemy at bay, but the wooden castles of Japan offered no such protection.

During the Keicho Era (1596) an attempt was made to make the castle walls thicker and stronger by a method called "*nurigomezukuri*". Layer upon layer of plaster was applied to the walls to thicken them. This followed the traditional method of the lacquer craftsman who applied his lacquer in the same manner allowing one layer to dry thoroughly before applying the next. Although this idea increased the fire-resistance and helped to make the castle less vulnerable in an attack, it could not eliminate the inherent weakness of the wooden structure.

This use of different construction materials was the basic difference between Japanese and Western castle construction, and in Japan it became evident that for defense purposes the wooden castle was far too vulnerable. As it was realized that the castle building itself had intrinsic weaknesses in time of war, it became increasingly clear that the problem of defense must be entrusted to strongly fortified outworks. Therefore, the strict ban on castle construction by the Tokugawa Shogunate (1615-1868) did not prohibit the construction of domestic buildings or other work unrelated to defense.

In contrast to this, the impregnable stone walls of Western castles made such elaborate outwork fortification unnecessary. In fact the plan of a Western castle is extremely simple in outline compared with a Japanese castle. Gothic style castles, for example, were often built on a hillock with only one middle bailey. One of this type of castles is Pierreford's in France built on a hillock, with the buildings surrounding one large middle bailey. The towers at each corner, and in the middle of each wall, were used to defend the castle. Generally speaking, many Western castles were built on these comparatively simple lines.

A Japanese castle, however, had numerous baileys built on various levels and surrounded by moats, or stone walls. In addition to the inner citadel, middle citadel and outer citadel, some castles had many baileys diversely arranged on various levels, leading up to the highest level on which the main donjon was built (see picture map). These baileys had various names and were eventually classified, but some were so complex they defied classification. This diversification of baileys developed from the middle of the 16th century.

[Picture Map of Himeji Castle] — In constructing these baileys the natural topography of the site was closely followed, and the baileys were constructed on flat hillocks or on hilltops flattened for the purpose. Stone walls were also built in strategic positions to strengthen the defenses. Until 1600 many castles were planned after this manner, but as castle construction underwent extensive changes, stone walls were used more widely and became an integral part of the castle's defense system.

In time, the choice of site for a castle moved from the summits of mountains to hill-tops and finally on to level ground. When castles were built on flat land, massive square stone wall bases were constructed and the baileys were built on top of these (see page 70). These stone walls were gradually developed for defense purposes as the wooden structure was so vulnerable in an attack.

Stone was also used to strengthen the castle entrance. Originally one entered the castle by a large wooden gate, but however impressively it displayed its coating of iron, it was not fire-resistant and it had all the weaknesses inherent in a wooden structure. An entrance itself is a vulnerable spot, and to remedy this the "masugata" gate was devised. The name "masugata" is derived from a square measuring box, called a masu, which was commonly used for measuring rice, beans, etc. Thus "masugata" means square-shaped. This gate area was a rectangular piece of ground surrounded by walls. The main gate was on an outer wall and a second gate on an adjacent wall to prevent the castle grounds from being seen from outside. On entering the main gate one stood in the rectangular walled courtyard, and on turning right (usually) and passing through the second gate, one entered the castle grounds. Some walls surrounding the "masugata" were made of dried mud, but in most castles stone was used for these walls, making this unique entrance more secure.

Using stone walls in these various ways gave the castle quite a different appearance after the Middle Ages. Such walls are peculiar to Japanese castles, and were probably not even considered in the West where the tradition had developed of building the actual castle of stone. It is, in fact, these stone walls, together with the specially diversified layout of the baileys and the castle architecture itself, that give such a unique appearance to a Japanese castle.

The stone used for Western castles was cut and shaped, which made any attempts to climb the castle walls difficult. In early Japanese castles, however, the stone walls were built with natural stones just as they were found; they were not broken or shaped in any way. Consequently the walls were not steep, and the crudely shaped stones offered easy footholds to would-be wallscalers; so the walls themselves did not provide full protection in an attack. They did, however, further complicate the already maze-like ground plan of the castle, and in this way hindered an enemy's attempt to approach the main donjon. As these stone walls were more closely integrated into the complicated planning of the castle, they were made to harmonize so well with the castle architecture that the total result was a castle of unparalled grandeur, and unique in its beauty.

The importance attached to stone walls as a means of defense is evidenced by the government's policy of not allowing them to be repaired, but construction of a general or domestic nature was allowed. Castle construction was strictly prohibited. Regulations regarding the repair of stone walls were very demanding. Government permission was necessary for each part of the wall to be repaired, and many documents, including detailed plans of each repair, had to be submitted for government inspection. It is from these documents that we have learned much about prevailing conditions in those times.

As stated above, the Japanese feudal lord's castle had a similar function to a Western feudal castle, but they were completely different in appearance. From earliest times they were both used for defense, but in the West this defensive power lay in the stone castle building itself, whereas in Japan it was developed in the outwork fortifications in an attempt to protect the wooden castle. Interestingly enough, as before mentioned, the fundamental difference was one of construction materials.

1. Main Citadel
2. Bizen Citadel
3. Middle Citadel
4. Outer Citadel
5. West Citadel
6. Main Donjon
7. Inner Moat
8. Gate A
9. Gate B
10. Gate C
11. Gate D
12. Gate E
13. Gate F
14. Gate G
15. Gate H
16. Gate I
17. Gate J
18. Gate K
19. Water Gate No.1
20. Water Gate No.5
21. Hishi Gate
22. Sangoku Moat

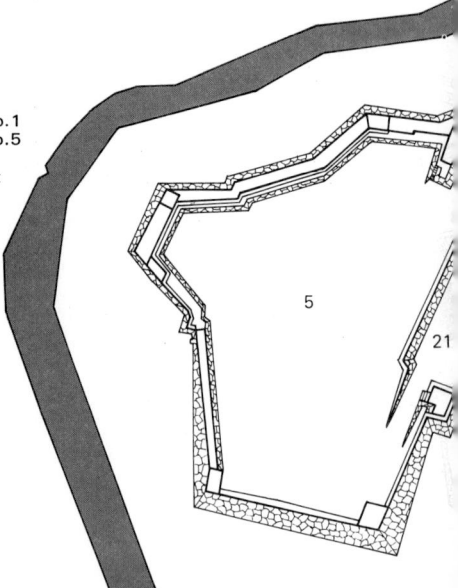

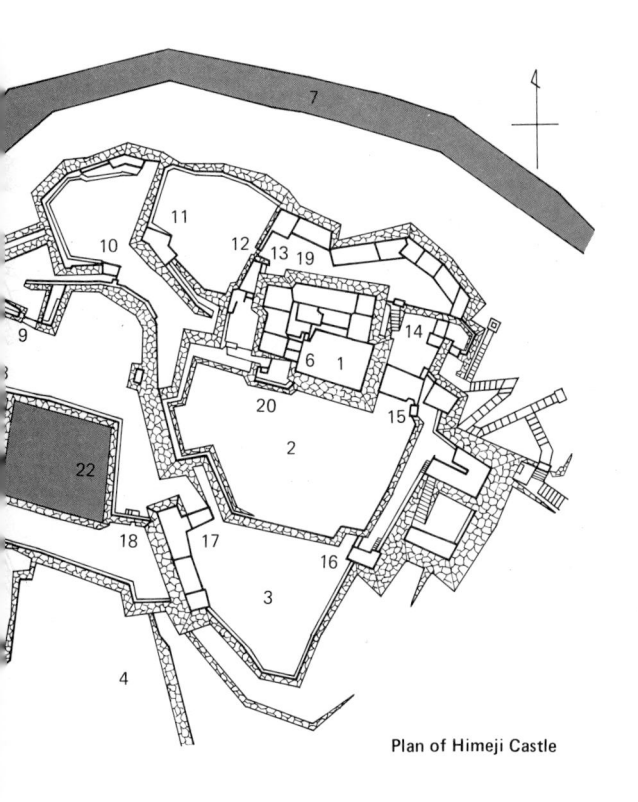

Plan of Himeji Castle

Outstanding Japanese Castles

Kumamoto Castle and Himeji Castle — It is said that wars enforce research and accelerate progress in military fields, and Japanese castles certainly made rapid strides forward at the time of the Sekigahara War (1600). From the Keicho era (1598) east and west Japan had split into two opposing factions, and in preparation for the anticipated war great progress was made in the fortification and development of castles. The policy was being pursued of defending the traditional wooden castle with a complicated system of outwork fortifications, and this war provided the opportunity for testing the effectiveness of this policy. These experiments ushered in the most prosperous era of Japanese castle construction and outwork fortification.

There are no castles remaining from the Tensho and Bunsho eras (1573-1595) and most modern castles, built after the Keicho era, have no old parts left. Matsumoto Castle, which was started in 1594 and completed about 1600, had "windows" for marksmen in all the walls, and there were many stone-throwing "windows" on the first floor. There were no living quarters in the main donjon; it was used as a store-house. Between this and the small donjon was a long horizontal turret called a "toro", in which they made an entrance gate. If an enemy approached this entrance it could be defended from both the main donjon and the small one. This is typical of the type of developement of fortification in castles at that time, but the progress made at the time of the Sekigahara War is best exemplified by Kumamoto Castle in Kyushu.

The master architect, Kiyomasa Kato, built Kumamoto Castle, and its construction was such as to well deserve its reputation as the most famous castle in Japan. Unfortunately it was not spared the bombing of World War II. Although so famous, it is not clear when it was built. Kiyomasa went to live in Kumamoto in 1588, but during the period 1592-1598 he was engaged in the Korean War and presumably had little time for castle planning. Until recently it was thought to have been completed in 1602, but the excavation of some roof tiles bearing the inscription, "August, Keicho 4th year (1600). Auspicious day", confirmed that it was finished just before the Sekigahara War. During recent reconstruction work it was discovered that the small donjon had been built as an extension in later years, so the inscribed tiles belonged to the main donjon and the small donjon must have been built after the Sekigahara War. This can be seen, too, from the difference in construction technique of both the stone walls and the donjon itself; therefore the two donjons belong to different periods.

When we consider the rather ungainly appearance of the main donjon when it stood alone, it probably gave the impression of a very early style castle. The whole of the first floor was built overhanging the stone wall base (page 32), so in an emergency they could take up the flooring in this section and use it as a stone-throwing area. This was not in the original planning, but was a later development.

In contrast, the small donjon was obviously designed to meet a war-time emergency and had facilities not to be found in the main donjon. A well, kitchen, and latrines, together with sufficient space for all the samurais to gather, enabled them to defend the castle from this small donjon in a last stand against an enemy. Such defense facilities indicate the great development in the fortification of castles at this period.

The supreme masterpiece of extant castle construction is undoubtedly to be found in Himeji Castle, which has a beauty and significance surpassing all other castles in Japan. This is not simply because most of the castle buildings are still intact; there are many other reasons why it is reputed to be Japan's most magnificent castle.

Perhaps the first reason is the grand scale on which it is built. Although it cannot be compared with the great castles of such powerful rulers as Hideyoshi Toyotomi or Ieyasu Tokugawa, it is the most outstanding castle of all the daimyos. The reason for this lies in the circumstances under which it was built.

After the Sekigahara War, Ieyasu Tokugawa, the victorious shogun, made a distribution of awards and changed the fiefs of many of the daimyos. The fiefs from the Edo (Tokyo) area extending west to the Kinki (Osaka) district were allotted to the hereditary Tokugawa daimyos who had been Ieyasu's retainers for many years. The more distant fiefs of western Honshu, Kyushu, and Shikoku were given to the non-hereditary daimyos who had received Toyotomi's patronage. The fief of Harima, which bordered these distant western fiefs, was Ieyasu's front line of defense against these western lords.

For meritorious service in the Sekigahara War, Terumasa Ikeda was given this strategically important fief, which yielded about two and a half million bushels of rice annually. Terumasa was a greatly trusted son-in-law of Ieyasu. Later, Terumasa's son married Ieyasu's grand-daughter, and this, too, strengthened the family ties so that finally Terumasa became a Governor-general with an annual stipend of five million bushels of rice. Hideyoshi Toyotomi had previously built Himeji Castle, but Terumasa completely remodelled it as a daimyo's residential castle. The work began in 1601, was completed in 1609, and millions of people were employed in the construction work.

Himeji is located mid-way between east and west Honshu, and it commands the rear approaches to Osaka and its castle which in those days was held by Hideyori Toyotomi. Defense of this advance guard position was all important to Ieyasu Tokugawa, so he gave every encouragement to Terumasa's castle building, and when we consider Terumasa's huge stipend it is understandable that he could build such a magnificent castle.

The second reason for Himeji's fame is that it was built at a time when the art of castle building was in its prime, and it incorporated the most advanced techniques of those times. The collective experience of ten years of civil war had developed both ideas and skills, and these were freely used and attained a level of consummate skill in Himeji Castle.

Amongst these advanced techniques, one of the most interesting is the extremely complicated nawabari, or ground plan, which is like a maze. If an enemy tried to attack the main donjon, on approaching it the road unexpectedly took a turn in the opposite direction and on making this turn the enemy were then fired upon from loopholes in the gate and walls. As explained in a later chapter, the complicated nawabari is peculiar to Japanese castles, but in only a few castles can one see this device used so elaborately as in Himeji.

A third noteworthy reason for Himeji Castle's importance is its contribution to the development of the art of castle construction. The beauty of the pure white chalkstone walls is indeed befitting the name White Heron Castle by which it is popularly known, and this method of plastering the walls was a technical advance which also made them fire-proof. The "nurigome" method of putting layer upon layer of plaster on the walls made them much more durable than the wooden boards with which they had previously been made, and they were even secure against the "fire arrows" which were used at that time.

A further advance was the application of this nurigome technique to the whole building which we can see in both Hagi and Himeji Castles. The low, over-hanging eaves in Japanese architecture are particularly dangerous in case of fire: flames leaping out of a window quickly set alight the wooden underside of such eaves causing the roof to burn and collapse. It was in Himeji Castle that for the first time consideration was given to using this nurigome technique on the underside of the eaves to make them fire-proof. In Kumamoto Castle the top floor had white wooden undereaves, but the other roofs were made of nurigome. In Himeji Castle the whole building was treated with this white nurigome. hence its comparison to a great white heron. Nowadays, these beautiful white walls are one of the things long remembered after visiting a Japanese castle.

Next we can also see evidence of architectural progress, for in Himeji castle's donjon alone they had perfected a building from which they could withhold a seige for a long period of time. The idea was also used in Kumamoto's small tower which has previously been described. The donjons of early castles were isolated and extremely vulnerable, so gradually they attached a look-out tower or a small donjon connected to the main donjon by a corridor. They also attempted to fortify the castle entrance which was specially vulnerable, but all these efforts were in vain if they lacked the necessary facilities to withstand an attack.

In the case of Himeji Castle three small donjons are connected by a corridor making one unit for use in time of seige. The three donjons surrounded an inner courtyard where they built a kitchen, and in the lowest donjon they stored salt. Water could not be neglected, and as there was no well in the courtyard they used the one in the Well Bailey which was very close by.

Wakayama Castle, destroyed by fire in World War II, was the first castle to have an inner courtyard designed like this. Asano Yukinaga built this castle after the Sekigahara War, and besides the main and small donjons, it also had two towers connected by a long horizontal turret called a Tamon (see page 87).

So it was that after the Sekigahara War the art of castle building reached its prime, and one result of this was the readiness of the samurais to hold the castle from the main donjon if beseiged.

The structure of the donjon is interesting too. Owing to the frequency of earthquakes in Japan it was essential to have some central unifying support running from top to bottom of high wooden buildings. Usually two huge central pillars extended from the basement to the floor of the top storey. Even today in a two storey house a supporting pillar is usually erected, but in a high building this unification is even more necessary.

In the very early Azuchi and Osaka Castle's donjons there were no known supporting columns, but in Inuyama Castle and Okayama Castle, which were destroyed by fire, thre were very thin supports. This was a serious defect in a high building. In Himeji Castle's main donjon two huge supporting pillars unify the whole structure, and other castles, built after Himeji, used this construction principle.

There are an unlimited number of structural details used in Himeji Castle which show evidence of architectural progress. To strengthen the castle entrance the leaves of the gate were completely covered with iron and stone throwing "windows" were built in the turret above the gate to ward off approaching enemies (page 48). In the section facing the inner courtyard of the main citadel, rows of windows were inserted to provide more light; a practical innovation for use in time of seige (page 49). The significance of Himeji Castle is that all these technically brilliant buildings and devices remain and are so well preserved that they make this the outstanding castle of Japan today.

During this period of castle development many ingenious military devices were incorporated in the construction, and many of these can be seen in Nagoya Castle which was built at the end of the Golden Age of castle construction. Building began in 1610, and with the approaching Osaka War work on the main donjon (popularly known as "golden dolphin", because the dolphins which topped the gables were painted gold) was hurried so that it was almost completed by December 1612. Regrettably, it was destroyed by fire in World War II. The stone wall base of the main donjon is important as the independent work of Kiyomasa Kato. The main donjon and the small donjon are connected by a bridge abutment (see page 70) and there are high stone walls on both sides of this. On the Western wall of the donjon they installed hidden loopholes and spiked walls. These defended the last big gateway, so preventing the enemy from approaching and passing through it into the inner citadel.

The hidden loopholes were built in the donjon walls but were covered over on the outside with a thin layer of plaster and painted like the wall. In an emergency the thin outer covering could be broken from inside and the enemy surprised by marksmen. The stone throwing windows, too, were inconspicuous from outside. Beneath the second floor gables is a protruding part of the wall which rests on the eaves of the first floor (picture page 37). This looks like an architectural design, but in fact the undereaves of the first floor open up and stones were thrown from this protruding area. Such concealed fortifications were called the "hidden claws." Although these can be seen as developments in military architecture, Nagoya Castle lacked the beauty of design of Himeji Castle, and many features pointed the way to the more austere donjons of the later Edo era.

Some of the features were the excessively curved corners of the eaves and the unimaginative grouping of the "hollow-eyed" windows. The fashionable copper lattice work on the roof gables may have been an innovation, but it did nothing to soften the rigid lines of the building, so that on the whole it lacked the gracious lines of Himeji Castle. And yet the completed installations inside the donjon were of the most progressive type. Amongst other things in the basement were a treasury, a rice granary, a well, and storeooms for military equipment for use in time of seige. These last were probably part of the careful preparations which Ieyasu Tokugawa diligently made prior to the Osaka War.

The Plan of Japanese Castles (Nawabari)

"Nawabari" is a word which indicates the entire level surface plan of a castle, and included use of the natural topography in planning the castle. Nowadays, the nawabari is a rope stretched out on the ground to mark the actual area where the castle is to be built, but in both cases it indicates the area where the construction work is done.

The nawabari is extremely important in a Japanese castle, and it is said that the art of nawabari as developed in Japan has no parallel in the world. As the wooden castles were very vulnerable in a war, the nawabari was one of the necessary devices developed to help defend the castle. Its development was the result of actual fighting experience extending over the long turbulent period of civil war, and most progress was made during this period.

As a general principle, later Japanese castles had a basic plan of an inner citadel (hon-maru), a middle citadel (ni-no-maru) and an outer citadel (san-no-maru), but besides these some castles had many other baileys. These were of infinite variety, their arrangement depending upon the topography of the site. Originally many medieval castles used a mountain-top position as a natural defense, but the arrangement of baileys was extremely irregular owing to the steep slopes of the mountain. Some were arranged in concentric circles, others in rows, but generally speaking in these early castles, the number of arrangements was limited when compared with later castles. With the development of firearms and the resulting change in methods of warfare, the arrangement of the baileys gradually became very complex and much larger in scale. Often a battle now depended on being able to muster the greater part of one's forces and attack, so a complicated nawabari was introduced in order to confuse an enemy who had penetrated into the castle grounds. It was the development and introduction of the massive stone walls at this point that contributed so much to making the planning of these baileys so complex.

In the hill castles of the Middle Ages theys used the topography of the site to the best of their ability, and in vulnerable places they built baileys on top of earthworks. Although these had defects they probably served their purpose of defending the castle. When the castle later moved to flatland and a hilltop position no longer offered defense possibilities, heavy stone walls became a necessity to help protect the main citadel and to form a base on which to build the baileys. Thus it was that the stone walls became indispensible in the development of the nawabari as explained previously.

This does not mean, however, that the choice of site became a secondary consideration. Sites continued to be chosen which offered maximum protection, and rivers, lakes or the sea were often utilized as moats. Takamatsu Castle and Karatsu Castle used the sea as a vast moat, while Takashima Castle in Nagano Prefecture and Zeze Castle integrated Lake Biwa and Lake Suwa into their defense plans. These were sometimes known as "fu-jo" or floating castles because they were completely surrounded by water. An even more common practice was to use a river as a defense line. The use of these natural features inevitably influenced the plan of the castle and caused many variations in the nawabari.

To be able to defend the castle with the least possible number of people was the ideal, so they favored a circular site. Such a site offered the smallest circumference for any given area, and it was possible to defend it with the least number of people. Such circular sites were a feature of foreign castles, but in Japan circular construction with wood and stone walls presented many problems. Tanaka Castle in Shizuoka Prefecture is an example of a circular castle. A square or rectangular site was also difficult to maintain owing to the use of the surrounding land features.

Dr. Orui classified the various types of nawabari into the following categories: rinkaku style, hashigokaku style and renkaku style.

The rinkaku style had the main citadel in the centre and the second and third citadels arranged in concentric circles around it. Although this may seem to be an ideal arrangement for defense of the main citadel, there are surprisingly few of this type of castle. There are two possible reasons. First, the moats and stone walls of such a castle were extremely long compared with the small area on which the main citadel was built. Second, even though ideal from the point of view of defense, such extensive earthwork took a maximum amount of time and labor making construction work both difficult and costly. Shizuoka and Tanaka castles follow this style, and Osaka, Utsunomiya, Yamagata and Mihara castles are also very similar.

Hashigokaku style had the main citadel as the apex and from this the second and third citadels descend in steps like a stairway. Typical of this style are Iiyama Castle, Iida Castle and Takayama Castle in Gifu Prefecture. There are also many such castles in Nagano Prefecture, and among the big castles, Hagi and Aizu-Wakamatsu Castles are also Hashigokaku style.

In this type of castle, the main citadel was in a very exposed position being built on the highest ground. This was

Plan of Tanaka Castle

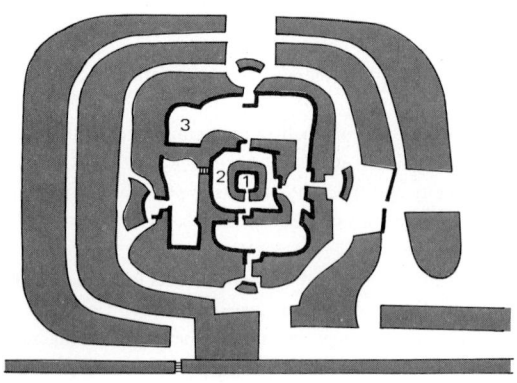

1. Main Citadel   2. Middle Citadel   3. Outer Citadel

a disadvantage defence-wise, and to compensate for this it was necessary to provide some form of natural defense such as a lake or a river to prevent ease of access. Iiyama Castle is situated at the junction of two rivers and the width of these natural moats offered much protection. There was no river near Takayama Castle but the main citadel was on a high mountain, the steep slopes of which made access very difficult. Such defense was reminiscent of castles built in the Middle Ages.

Renkaku style had the main citadel in the center with the second and third citadels on either side. Three castles of this type are Nagaoka, Mito and Sendai.. In this style, too, it was necessary to provide some kind of protection for the exposed main citadel.

These three nawabari styles are the basis on which the various styles of castles were built after the Middle Ages. The mountain castle was restricted in design by the very nature of

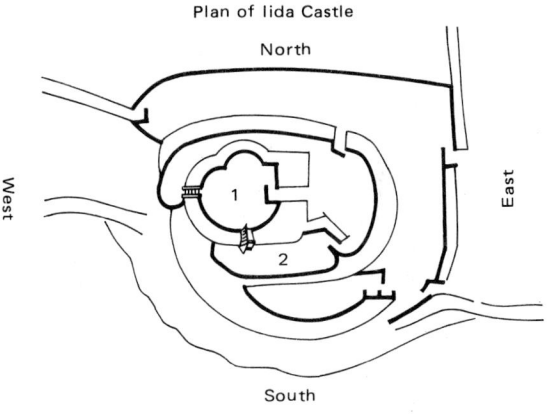

Plan of Iida Castle

1. Main Castle   2. Southern Bailey

its site, but the nawabari of a castle on flat land could be designed with greater flexibility, although use of the natural land features tended to produce a castle irregular in shape. The hill castle was more irregular, of course, as the shape of the main citadel was determined by the shape of the mountain.

To summarise, the essential function of the nawabari was to provide defense for the main citadel and eventually this resulted in a nawabari which was labyrinth-like in its complexity.

Let us now take a detailed look at the complicated nawabari of Himeji Castle.

Himeji Castle's Nawabari

Built on the Plains of Harima, Himeji Castle has the peaks of the central Honshu mountain ranges as a northern backdrop. To the south runs the coastline of the famed Inland Sea. Eastwards it is bordered by the Ichi River and on the west by the Yumesaki River. Mt. Hime, is only about 46 metres above sea level, so it could not be considered a natural defense. It was dominated on the south by the high Mt. Keifukuji and on the west by Mt. Otoko.

In 1601 when Terumasa Ikeda built the castle, he first diverted the flow of the Ichi River and made a dike. Then after clearing the land, the earthworks were begun. With Mt. Hime at the centre, the castle spread over a wide area to the east, south and north, but the land narrowed in the west. The whole castle was encircled by a spiral shaped moat, and from the foot of Mt. Hime three baileys were constructed. The main citadel was surrounded by the second, third and west citadels. Beyond these lay the middle baileys and outer baileys. At first sight they appeared like concentric circles, but in fact the inner, middle and outer moats formed a spiral. In this way it resembled Edo Castle.

Nowadays the outer baileys are practically nonexistent, but when it was built this was where the prison and the firearms practice area were located. The samurai houses, and the foot soldiers and merchants quarters were also in these outer baileys. Now the middle moat has been almost completely filled in except for parts remaining on the north, east and west sides. Tourists visiting the castle usually see the inner bailey only, but even from this alone one can see the ingenious planning. Covering an area of 276, 000 sq. yds. this inner bailey is almost circular with masugata style entrances on the east and south sides. A smaller entrance was on the southeast side. The south and east were most suitable for entrances as the northern and western slopes of Himeyama are steep and limit the actual castle area.

The southern gate, the Sakura Gate, was used by high ranking visitors, and the eastern gate, the Kisei Gate, was the postern gate.

Between the west and main citadels there is an emergency exit. This is a shortcut going to the Sagiyamaguchi Gate with steps from the gate to the foot of the mountain. In Wakayama Castle there is a similar type of emergency exit. This started at the main donjon's kitchen entrance and led north, but a sudden detour brought one to a southern gate very quickly. The Sakura Gate of Himeji Castle is especially noteworthy as it has a double masugata gate. Besides the impressive outer gate, there were two inner gates known as Paulownia (tree's name) No. 1, and No. 2 gates. This construction of three gates at the entrance cannot be seen in any other castle. On passing through the third gate one entered the third citadel in which was located the lord's main palace, and this probably explains why the Sakura Gate was so well protected.

During Terumasa Ikeda's time the lord's palace had been in the main citadel, but when Honba succeeded Ikeda after the Osaka Wars, he ordered many additional structures. Among these were the building of the lord's palace in the third citadel and the famous Musashino Palace for Princess Sen (Senhime), Ieyasu's beautiful granddaughter.

On proceeding north through the third citadel we come to the Hishi (waterchestnut, or diamond shape) Gate which leads us into the second citadel. From the Hishi Gate the layout of the castle is very complex and demonstrates well the complex nawabari which is peculiar to Himeji Castle. From the Hishi Gate there are two routes leading to the main donjon: the upper route and the lower route. On the upper route there are four gates, A, B, C and D.

From Gate A, one can go to the main donjon by the lower route. This route skirts the southern edge of the Bizen Citadel (now called the main citadel) and has four gates too: L, J, I and H. From the Hishi Gate, however, there is a direct path which joints the lower route at Gate J. On this path one passes through Gate K which is just a small opening made in a wall. This is called the Uzumi Gate, which can be translated as Concealed Gate, a most suitable name, as from a distance it is difficult to see the gate at all.

Should an enemy gain entrance, reach the Hishi Gate, and proceed to Gate A, on the right is the remains of a moat known as Sangoku (three countries) Moat, and on the left are the clean lines of the west citadel's stone wall. The path leading to Gate A between this wall and the moat is very narrow so it was very easy to attack the enemy's flank from the west citadel, and drive them out. Since Gate B is close to Gate A, flank attacks could be made at this point. On entering Gate B, the road forks: the left fork leads into the west citadel itself, but the right fork leads along an extremely narrow path to Gate C. One of the famous features of the complexity of Himeji Castle's nawabari is that at this point (Gate C) the main donjon seems to be almost at touching distance, and yet the castle layout is so ingenious an enemy could not easily find the right approach to it. Another deterrent to any would-be intruder were the loopholes on the top of the left-hand wall of the narrow approach to Gate C. From these an enemy could be attacked when passing along the narrow path.

After passing through Gate C, the tower of Gate D and the white mud wall approaching it face us in a northeastern direction. The route goes east, comes to a dead end, then an enemy must turn around and facing them is a hill with Gate D at the top. At this point the castle layout is again most complex. It resembles a maze and would defeat the most persistent enemy (p. 44). Although this hill road is situated immediately before the main donjon, an enemy again had to go straight as far as they could, take a 180° turn, and then find themselves facing Gate D. The whole approach was covered by loopholes from the walls of the upper part of the North West Tower. The route was so labyrinth-like that enemy had neither time to rest nor a chance to escape, and this ingenious planning, together with the various kinds of loopholes scattered over the area makes Himeji Castle unique among Japanese Castles. Such devices point to the fact that Himeji was built when the art of castle building in Japan was at its highest.

Continuing along the upper route from Gate D one enters a rather large North-West bailey. On the east side of this is Gate E and on passing through this gate one finally reaches the main citadel. An enemy approaching through Gate E would probably rush forward along the route going east between the main donjon and the long, low towers on the north side. However, if they continued along this route they would come to Gate F which leads to the postern gate, and the main citadel would be bypassed.

In order to enter the main citadel after passing through Gate E one must turn sharp right and enter the small gate called No. 1 Water Gate (Page 45). From this point the number of gates gradually increases. One passes through No. 2, 3 and 4 Water Gates, and reaches the main donjon through the 5th Water Gate. The distance between these gates is so small that they resemble a series of masugata gates. Should an enemy delay in this area, they could be attacked from the tops of the surrounding small donjons. There is no other castle which uses this kind of device as a means of defense. Iyo-Matsuyama Castle is somewhat similar but it is worth noting that all the ideas used in both castles were conceived during Keicho era which was the prosperous age of castle building.

The series of Water Gates illustrates the prevalence of symbolism in Japanese thought in those days. The character for water was often inscribed on buildings as a protection against fire. It was believed that such a character had the effect of symbolically turning the inscribed wall into water, thus preventing it from catching fire. In this way the series of water gates protected the main donjon.

The lower route, which branches off from Gate A, is not nearly so complex as the upper route described above, but it is specially fortified. Gate L was destroyed by fire during the Meiji era, but the path just in front of Gate J forms a right angle making an area like a masugata gate. Above Gate J are two long turrets which extend over the gate and these are more strongly fortified than any such turrets on the upper route.

On entering Gate J one passes through the upper hilly area

122

at the foot of the Bizen Citadel until one reaches Gate I. This gate has a Taiko (Drum) Tower on the right side, and on the left the stone wall forms a right angle making another masugata which is so small it was impossible for a large number of invaders to attack. On passing through Gate I there lies a narrow passageway, called the East Side Bailey. This is flanked on the left by the high stone wall of the Bizen Citadel and on the right it overlooks the precipitious stone walls of the Harakiri Bailey. Hemmed between these, an intruder could go neither right nor left, and advancing, would reach the Well Tower. On the left of this tower is the Bizen Gate which leads to the Bizen Citadel, now part of the main citadel. The castle layout in front of the Bizen Gate is somewhat complex. At the side of the Well Tower is an old guard box and beside this is Gate H which leads down a path of twisting steps to the postern gate. Thus, the lower route and the pathway from the postern gate meets at Bizen Gate. However, to reach the central citadel one must pass Gate H, go around the north side of the main citadel, and eventually one is on the upper route and can enter from the 1st Water Gate.

The Obi Tower is also in front of the Bizen Gate and below this to the south is a small bailey surrounded by stone walls and the Tamon tower. At the base of the stone walls is a tunnel-like path which passes under the Obi Tower and leads to the outer bailey. There is a well in this Well Bailey, hence its name, but now it is commonly called the Suicide Bailey. The origin of this name is not clear, but this is the well which was used when the main donjon did not have a well.

The Postern Gate of the castle is from the East Kisei Gate to the 4th C Gate. On passing through the latter the path zigzags steeply up the mountain side as far as the 2nd G Gate. The pathway is extremely steep, but the distance very short.

The stone wall in front of the 2nd G Gate is right-angled forming a masugata style gate, and on top of the wall is Ikaku Tower. Going through the 2nd G Gate, also known as Korai Gate, the slope is so steep that stone steps have been built, and Tower Gate is a perfect masugata style. The stone steps are built in a succession of short, twisting intervals like a spiral, and they are strongly defended from each gate. If we pass through 1st G Gate we are already in a part of the central citadel and on continuing to the left we find Gate H which leads to Bizen Gate. If we go right after 1st G Gate we reach Gate F and the northern side of the donjon, and we are then approaching the entrance to the donjon. Really, the 1st G Gate is an important link in the chain of fortifications which surround the main citadel. In the west is the main donjon, and small east donjon. The south is enclosed by encircling towers, and the north by protective walls. The planning is so remarkable that an enemy could be cut down from whatever direction they tried to attack.

Another interesting part of the castle is the West Bailey. This is the large section to the west of the Hishi Gate. It is not known what buildings were located there during Ikeda's residency, but the Honda family had the famous Kesho-yagura (cosmetic or ladies tower) built for Princess Sen. The living quarters of the chief ladies-in-waiting stretched around the perimeter of this bailey making a series of gracious buildings such as cannot be seen in any other castle.

Such a perfected system of defense, together with the graceful lines of the roofs, the long white walls, and the magnificent scale of the castle, puts Himeji Castle amongst the world's most famous castles.

HOIKUSHA COLOR BOOKS

ENGLISH EDITIONS

Book Size 4″×6″

① KATSURA
② TOKAIDO HIROSHIGE
③ EMAKI
④ KYOTO
⑤ UKIYOE
⑥ GEM STONES
⑦ NARA
⑧ TOKYO Past and Present
⑨ KYOTO GARDENS
⑩ IKEBANA
⑪ KABUKI
⑫ JAPANESE CASTLES
⑬ JAPANESE FESTIVALS
⑭ WOOD-BLOCK PRINTING
⑮ N O H
⑯ HAWAII
⑰ JAPAN
⑱ BUDDHIST IMAGES
⑲ OSAKA
⑳ HOKUSAI
㉑ ORIGAMI
㉒ JAPANESE SWORDS
㉓ GOLDFISH
㉔ SUMI-E
㉕ SHELLS OF JAPAN
㉖ FOLK ART
㉗ TOKYO NIKKO FUJI
㉘ NATIONAL FLAGS
㉙ BONSAI
㉚ UTAMARO
㉛ TEA CEREMONY
㉜ PAPER DOLLS
㉝ CERAMICS
㉞ MODEL CARS
㉟ CREATIVE ORIGAMI
㊱ Z E N
㊲ KIMONO
㊳ CHINESE COOKING
㊴ KYOGEN
㊵ NOH MASKS
㊶ LIVING ORIGAMI
㊷ SHINKANSEN
㊸ OSAKA CASTLE
㊹ BUNRAKU
㊺ TOKYO SUBWAYS

COLORED ILLUSTRATIONS FOR NATURALISTS

Text in Japanese, with index in Latin or English.

Book Size 6″ × 8″

1. BUTTERFLIES of JAPAN
2. INSECTS of JAPAN vol.1
3. INSECTS of JAPAN vol.2
4. SHELLS of JAPAN vol.1
5. FISHES of JAPAN vol.1
6. BIRDS of JAPAN
7. MAMMALS of JAPAN
8. SEA SHORE ANIMALS of JAPAN
9. GARDEN FLOWERS vol.1
10. GARDEN FLOWERS vol.2
11. ROSES and ORCHIDS
12. ALPINE FLORA of JAPAN vol.1
13. ROCKS
14. ECONOMIC MINERALS
15. HERBACEOUS PLANTS of JAPAN vol.1
16. HERBACEOUS PLANTS of JAPAN vol.2
17. HERBACEOUS PLANTS of JAPAN vol.3
18. SEAWEEDS of JAPAN
19. TREES and SHRUBS of JAPAN
20. EXOTIC AQUARIUM FISHES vol.1
21. MOTHS of JAPAN vol.1
22. MOTHS of JAPAN vol.2
23. FUNGI of JAPAN vol.1
24. PTERIDOPHYTA of JAPAN
25. SHELLS of JAPAN vol.2
26. FISHES of JAPAN vol.2
27. EXOTIC AQUARIUM FISHES vol.2
28. ALPINE FLORA of JAPAN vol.2
29. FRUITS
30. REPTILES and AMPHIBIANS of JAPAN
31. ECONOMIC MINERALS vol.2
32. FRESHWATER FISHES of JAPAN
33. GARDEN PLANTS of the WORLD vol.1
34. GARDEN PLANTS of the WORLD vol.2
35. GARDEN PLANTS of the WORLD vol.3
36. GARDEN PLANTS of the WORLD vol.4
37. GARDEN PLANTS of the WORLD vol.5
38. THE FRESHWATER PLANKTON of JAPAN
39. MEDICINAL PLANTS of JAPAN

40. VEGETABLE CROPS of JAPAN
41. FARM ANIMALS of JAPAN
42. FUNGI of JAPAN vol.2
43. SHELLS of the WORLD vol.1
44. SHELLS of the WORLD vol.2
45. THE MARINE PLANKTON of JAPAN
46. EARLY STAGES of JAPANESE MOTHS vol.1
47. EARLY STAGES of JAPANESE MOTHS vol.2
48. FOSSILS
49. WOODY PLANTS of JAPAN vol.1
50. WOODY PLANTS of JAPAN vol.2
51. BRYOPHYTES of JAPAN
52. LICHEN FLORA of JAPAN
53. NATURALIZED PLANTS of JAPAN
54. DISEASES and PESTS of CULTIVATED TREES and SHRUBS
55. DISEASES and PESTS of FLOWERS and VEGETABLES
56. WAKAN-YAKU vol.1
57. WAKAN-YAKU vol.2
58. Coloured Guide of Wild Herbs with Artificial Key to Their Families
59. THE NEW ALPINE FLORA of JAPAN vol. I
60. THE NEW ALPINE FLORA of JAPAN vol. II
61. THE LAND SNAILS of JAPAN
62. JAPANESE CRUSTACEAN DECAPODS and STOMATOPODS vol. I
63. JAPANESE CRUSTACEAN DECAPODS and STOMATOPODS vol. II
64. THE LIFE HISTORIES OF BUTTERFLIES IN JAPAN vol. I
65. THE LIFE HISTORIES OF BUTTERFLIES IN JAPAN vol. II
66. THE LIFE HISTORIES OF BUTTERFLIES IN JAPAN vol. III
67. THE LIFE HISTORIES OF BUTTERFLIES IN JAPAN vol. IV
68. THE COLEOPTERA OF JAPAN vol. I
69. THE COLEOPTERA OF JAPAN vol. II
70. THE COLEOPTERA OF JAPAN vol. III
71. THE COLEOPTERA OF JAPAN vol. IV
72. Colored Illustrations of The Marine Fishes of Japan Vol. I
73. Colored Illustrations of The Marine Fishes of Japan Vol. II
74. SPIDERS OF JAPAN IN COLOR
75. Colored Illustrations of Mushrooms of Japan Vol. I
76. Colored Illustrations of Mushrooms of Japan Vol. II
77. Ornamental Tropical Plants of the World Vol. I

<ENGLISH EDITIONS>

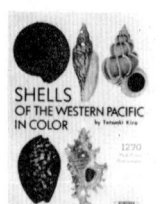

SHELLS OF THE WESTERN PACIFIC IN COLOR

Book Size 7″×10″

⟨vol. I⟩ by Tetsuaki Kira
(304 pages, 72 in color)
⟨vol. II⟩ by Tadashige Habe
(304 pages, 66 in color)

FISHES OF JAPAN IN COLOR

Book Size 7″×10″

by Toshiji Kamohara
(210 pages, 64 in color)